THE GIRL WITH THE
GREEN VIOLIN

KIRBY WRIGHT

More books available from:

Etched Press
www.etchedpress.com

Also available on Amazon Kindle

First Edition
Book Design by Kevin Dublin
Banda font by Typedepot

for Darcy

ACKNOWLEDGMENTS

I wish to thank the editors and staff of the following publications in which some of these poems first appeared or are forthcoming: *82 Review, Brickplight, The Broadkill Review, Emerge Literary Journal, Empty Mirror, FLARE: The Flagler Review, Foliate Oak Literary Magazine, Fox Cry Review, Gravel, Line Zero, Marco Polo Arts Magazine, Meat for Tea: The Valley Review, Poetic Diversity, Poetry Quarterly, The Prose-Poem Project, Santa Fe Literary Review, SHOUT OUT UK and Wilderness House Literary Review.

TABLE OF CONTENTS

Poem for a Poet	1
Once Immortal	2
Summer Town	3
At Crater Lake, Oregon	4
The Great Oak	5
The Monster in the House	6
House With Dragon Trees	7
The Woman in the Black One Piece	8
Son of Crab	9
Oceanside Beach	10
At Fat Albert's, Sellwood	12
Buccaneer Park	13
30 Years Between Letters	14
At the Coffee House	15
The Last Aztec Mocha	16
The Girl With the Green Violin	17

POEM FOR A POET

These days I find blood
In strange places,

Drops falling like rain
Staining the carpet.

I remember the razor dragging,
Unzipping me from myself.

Why do I plant
The arms and legs of dolls

In the earth
Of the redwood planter?

It amuses you.
I know.

Am I planting myself?
My only pictures of you

Are on the flaps of books.
You search for women

To belong to
When you know, deep down,

You belong to me
Or at least the part of me

That makes you hunger
For more bloody morsels.

Once Immortal

Enough future for us both.
You could see it looking east.
Here, take my body.
I bloom with memories of you.

You could see it looking east.
Remember undressing in mirrors.
I bloom with memories of you.
Your teeth white as pearls.

Remember undressing in mirrors.
I collect water from the roof for tea.
Your teeth white as pearls.
Drinking rain slows the hours.

Consider the tragedy of pouring.
Here, take my body.
My best years are behind me.
Enough future for us both.

My street? Strip of yellow lawns, oil-stained driveways, For Sale signs. A girl without eyes stares out the neighboring window. Asphalt shatters in the cul-de-sac. Women push strollers past a popped beach ball skinning the gutter blue.

I'm knotted in apron frosting a cake. The room for entertaining fills with strangers. Most seem older. I recall photo albums stacked in the garage beside the bag of charcoal. When I was young I was way above average. Grandpa toasts—wine glasses rise. Who are these people? Outside, sun scorches the drive.

At Crater Lake, Oregon

This blue is beyond cobalt,
the color of Earth's oceans
viewed from Mars.

Dip your wine glass
into the lake.
Sip the melt.

No rivers in.
No rivers out.
Whatever arrives stays.

What mysterious currents
send Llao's Fingers
west from eastern shore?

Pines root the cliffs.
Trout rise to taste
volcanic dust.

White pelicans claim
the emerald pool
on Wizard Island.

Break off
a sprig of hemlock.
Open the soft needles.

Smell a hundred centuries
as the branches sway,
revealing the moon.

Note:
Llao's Fingers: patterns on the surface caused by the spirit of the slain god of the
lake

It was a scorching summer and the great oak was dying. Ferns drowned in a cascade of leaves. Frogs fled. Birds didn't land on the bare branches. A boy tied a leaf to a pole and held it up to shade a bough. "It's the least I can do," he thought. The boy knew the great oak had provided shade for years, maybe even centuries, and it was time to give back. Children playing in the forest saw the boy and spread the word: all the boys and girls in the village started searching for poles. When the poles ran out they searched for sticks. Soon the great oak was sheltered from the sun. A girl raised her voice in song and the children joined in. Leaves quit falling as the great oak listened.

The Monster in the House

The hate in him keeps him alive.
As a child he was studious and loved challenges.
Sucking marrow from bone became his specialty.
He beats the oldest to break the others.

As a child he was studious and loved challenges.
Wife retreats to kitchen during the tortures.
He beats the oldest to break the others.
He's a lawyer feasting on children.

Wife retreats to kitchen during the tortures.
Lying upsets him most because he's a liar.
He's a lawyer feasting on children.
Neighbors pretend to hear and see nothing.

He wants you to fear him.
Sucking marrow from bone became his specialty.
His mother made her mother raise him.
The hate in him keeps him alive.

HOUSE WITH DRAGON TREES

The sun warms this morning before Easter, paralyzing cats in windows. "Pop Goes the Weasel" plays. Tiny feet chatter chasing an ice cream truck. There was a neighborhood below the volcano. I see a house with dragon trees, a net above the garage, backyard swings.

I return to bed. Teary Eary, my plush dog, remembers. See the boy run on cuts legs. Hear a soprano howl as the belt sings. Smell the iron scent of blood. Teary's fur is worn from hugging and biting.

At twilight, I rise and float ghost-like over the driveway. The children are gone. Popsicle sticks lie in the gutter. I flip the mailbox lid to find a bomb inside—an Easter card from Dadio.

7

THE WOMAN IN THE BLACK ONE PIECE

She crosses legs on the lounge chair,
rests the book on her belly.
She smoothes lotion
over arms and shoulders.
Funny how skin learns
pink instead of copper.
Men sleep in Speedos
on the other side of the pool.
She knows she's invisible
even to the man wheeling
a canvas cart, stuffing it with towels.
She contemplates the pool—
her pain goes deeper
than twelve feet under the board.
Axes have swung at her soul.

> No Lifeguard on Duty:
> Swim at Your Own Risk.

She treats wounds
with fantasy and chocolate.
She hears newlyweds
giggling inside the Jacuzzi,
recalls the aftermath
of a quilt spread
beside the picnic river.
The morning of stained glass promises
she believed, she really believed.
She slips on her glasses
and arrives at a Tuscan villa.
An Italian with a mustache
parachutes into the heroine's life.
She studies a sky too blue,
too deep to be real.

I am a sick man lying on a twin bed listening to rain. I have learned cold showers in a solar house inhabited by crabs. Dadio crab sits in a wheelchair clicking his remote. Mummy crab devours mahi-mahi out of a doggie bag. I have the maid's room. The maid left years ago. The crabs go to bed at midnight, him in his hospital bed with a view of the red ti garden, her in the king they once shared. They would claw one another when the salmon curtains were drawn. Now they scuttle through the house searching for water, entertainment, dead things to eat. Outside, rain floods the street. My skin hardens as I write.

Oceanside Beach

Pink and yellow umbrellas
Frost the foggy sand.

Surfers in wetsuits
Bob like apples

In a green-gray stew.
Sails fatten with wind.

Delicious bikinis patrol the strand.
The Beach Boys croon from a bungalow.

Two girls for every boy,
A woman for every man.

Toddlers toy with plastic shovels
While margaritas are sipped

From cans. The celebration goes for miles.
The marine layer gets assaulted

By the noonish sun—
Waves will turn jade

In less than an hour.
When I was younger

The beach seemed warmer.
Sir, have you seen my wife?

Legs churning north in aqua shorts?
Surging foam picks up clumps of kelp,

Tumbleweeds them over the sand.
Checkered black and yellow flags

Warn of currents and tragic undertows.
Sun ignites our faces—

We're exposed
Like drunks at a bar ready to close.

Happy birthday, Dadio. I'm playing counter kid in memory of you at this greasy spoon. I squeak on my vinyl stool and toy with a paper napkin. I try folding it into an angel. You'd tell me to act my age. My counter mates? A model-thin blonde in a Reed College sweatshirt and a bald man thumbing The Oregonian. The stink of fried eggs makes me nauseous. The waitress slides over a menu—she's doubling as the cook. I contemplate specials as steam fogs my cup.

Moments of indecision always summon you. "Learn to be decisive," you barked. I was your thorn, a chronic pain infected by the disgust of never making you proud. "Worthless," you mumbled one New Year's Eve. I learned defeat in our closed-door sessions, when screams and I'm-sorry-Daddy's joined the beat of the belt. I touched my wall and felt sorrow moving in waves through the redwood.

I vow to quit remembering. Memories send me beyond blue, into the indigo sky before twilight. Dadio, you carried hate into the hospital bed, where I spoon-fed you vanilla pudding and rubbed your feet under the sheets. Cold feet, I thought, icy heart. A nurse checked your pulse. "No more flowers," you scolded when my Christmas anthuriums arrived. I swore you'd never die but, if you did, I'd lug you like an overstuffed suitcase into the future.

A coffee refill comes—steam rises like a ghost. The blonde leaves and I crumple the angel napkin. The bald man retreats to the restroom. I feel as if I'm not human at all but a cold-blooded creature propped on a stool. The truth? Dadio, I've been shaped by you, folded by a lifetime of disappointment into a wrinkled toad.

BUCCANEER PARK

Palms sway like drunks
Along the Oceanside boardwalk.

Summer's gone.
Windows at Sam's Snack Shop

Are boarded up.
Two boys tug of war

A green boogie board.
A crow rips into a bag

In the beer bottle trash.
A girl moans

Inside a rocking van.
Smell blood on the wind?

Her cry is thirteen,
Fourteen tops.

A man yanks his collared golden
Down to the sand.

I could die on a day like this,
Sunny wind at 3 pm

On a Sunday losing at halftime
A gun held to my head.

30 Years Between Letters

Words from an old flame
Sunrise the past

The time of immortality
When the future

Was not reduced
But expansive as ocean

At sunset
Where you embraced

In a green flash
You would never see again

And believed in fire
Beyond the sea of shadows.

AT THE COFFEE HOUSE

She stands beside the doorway watching him wait in line with his old college buddy. "Tall Americano," he orders. He wears the aqua shorts she picked out to show off his butt and a dobby hat to hide the salt in his hair. There are girls behind him, coeds really, and he starts flirting. A blonde with hair past her waist giggles at something he says. The old college buddy joins in and it becomes a party. So many smiles, so much flashing of teeth. She steps back into twilight. She doesn't want coffee or cheesecake. It's something they do as a couple but the old college buddy makes her feel like a third wheel. She sits at a brick fire pit on the patio. The flames are orange and green. She spots him through glass—he clutches a venti-sized cup and performs exaggerated gestures like a silent movie star. The blonde is smiling. She hears the old college buddy's machinegun laugh. She kicks off her slippers. She swings bare feet up on brick, toes reaching for fire.

She announces to baristas and locals at the coffee bar that this will be her last Aztec Mocha for a year because she's off to Hanalei Bay tomorrow morning. There's an avalanche of hugs and tears. She wants to be missed. And she will be missed for her purchases and tapping out of caffeine-inspired monologues on the chocolate floor.

There will be no applause when she returns in twelve months. No one will admire her strings of puka shells, sniff her pikake perfume, or ask if Kauai's waters are warm. The familiars will have moved on to new hangouts and jobs as she waits for her final Aztec Mocha in a bar filled with strangers.

Notes:
puka: hole
pikake: Arabian jasmine

THE GIRL WITH THE GREEN VIOLIN

She is the band to me,
A splash of blonde on brown bangs,

Hair spilling to shoulders,
Small hand gliding bow over strings.

She stands under lights
At the edge of the stage

Firing song through a pub
Smelling of whiskey and stout.

Wall to wall men stand spellbound.
Fingers stroke the violin's neck.

She is an angel in denim
And mint sweater

Coaxing demons from a fiddle
Glowing Celtic emerald.

She summons the ghosts.
She finds the boy in me—

I am a man buried in debt
Bewitched back to the surface

By strings. I ache to jig her
Across the beer-stained floor

Through double doors
Until my skin burns

With blood moon.
I want a stone cottage

Overlooking the sea,
Sheep grazing my rise,

And the girl with the green violin
Playing forever beside me.